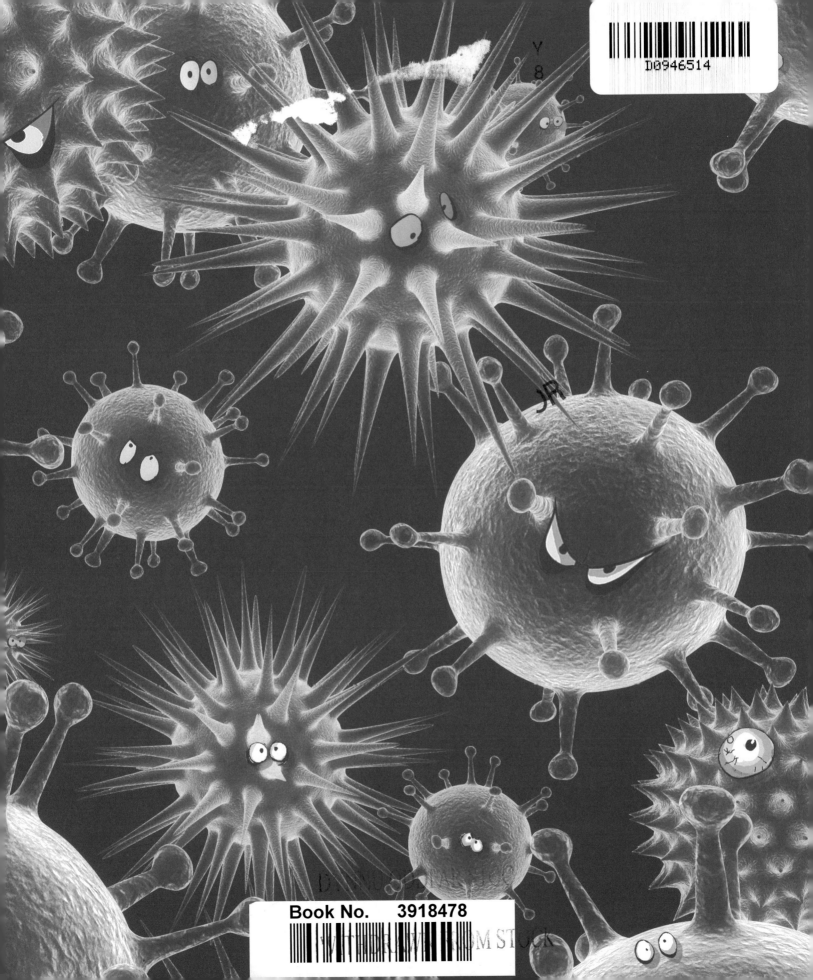

Y
8

D0946514

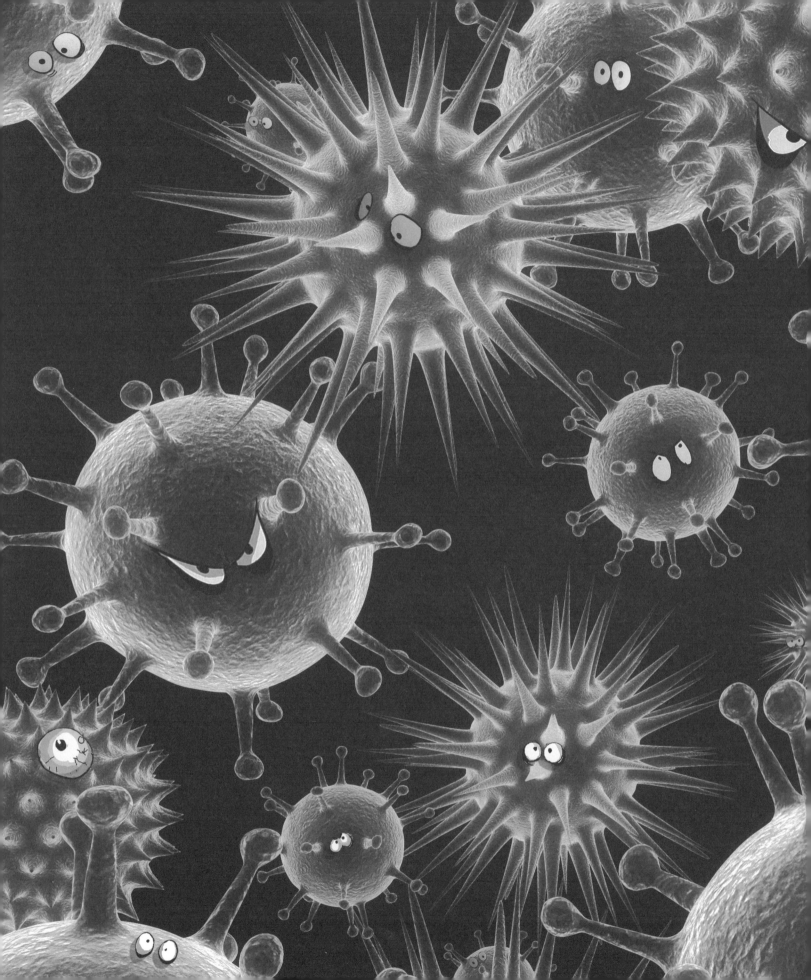

Plagues, Pox and Pestilence

Written by
Richard Platt

Illustrated by
John Kelly

KINGFISHER

KINGFISHER

First published 2011 by Kingfisher
an imprint of Macmillan Children's Books
a division of Macmillan Publishers Limited
20 New Wharf Road, London N1 9RR
Basingstoke and Oxford
Associated companies throughout the world
www.panmacmillan.com

**Consultant: Selina Hurley, Assistant Curator
of Medicine, Science Museum, London**

Concept and Design: Jo Connor

ISBN 978-0-7534-3168-9

3 5 7 9 8 6 4
3TR/1011/WKT/UNTD/140MA

A CIP catalogue record for this book
is available from the British Library.

Printed in China

This book is produced in association with the Science Museum.
Sales of this product support the Science Museum's
exhibitions and programmes.

Internationally recognized as one of the world's leading science
centres, the Science Museum, London, contains more than 10,000
amazing exhibits, two fantastic simulator rides and the astounding
IMAX cinema. Enter a world of discovery and achievement,
where you can see, touch and experience real objects and icons
which have shaped the world we live in today or visit
www.sciencemuseum.org.uk to find out more.

CONTENTS

DYNNU ODDI AR STOC

Dr Scratch
(a flea)

UNKNOWN
GERMS

Professor
Ratticus

LOOK OUT FOR THESE
CHARACTERS – THEY ARE
YOUR GUIDES THROUGH
THE DARK CORRIDORS
OF THE POX LAB

Lab assistant Mozzy
(a mosquito)

Lab assistant Tik-Tik
(a tsetse fly)

EBOLA
VIRUS

TUBER-
CULOSIS

WHAT ABOUT THESE POXY DATES IN THE BOOK?
CE: this means 'Common Era', the period
of measured time that begins with 1CE
(or 1AD). BCE: this means 'Before Common
Era', and refers to any dates before 1CE.
For example, 100BCE means '100 years
before the Common Era'.

IN THE POX LAB

Do you dare step inside the Pox Lab? In here, we study the history of the world's most horrible diseases. Catch one, and you will be very sick indeed. Or perhaps worse. Many of these dangerous illnesses spread quickly. Then thousands of people sicken and die in what we call an epidemic, a pestilence or a plague. But DO NOT PANIC!! We also study how we can stop deadly diseases today.

UNKNOWN GERMS

EBOLA VIRUS

TUBER-CULOSIS

History's epidemic villains

Germs do not always spread disease on their own. Some of them get a bit of help. Black rats, for example, spread bubonic plague (see pages 14 to 17). And the black rats get help, too. It is the fleas on the rats' backs that actually pass on the plague bacteria, known to us scientists as Yersinia pestis.

Rats spread more than 40 other human diseases, but they are not the only animal villains out there. Mosquitoes, snails, birds and even dogs and cats also carry illnesses. See how many carriers of disease you can spot as you tour the POX LAB.

Professor Ratticus

PLAGUE

PICK YOUR GERM

Just 150 years ago, people thought bad smells spread disease. Now we know that it is germs that cause illness. There are three kinds. Protists are tiny living creatures. Bacteria are simpler, and tinier still: they are the smallest known living things. Viruses are even smaller, but they are not alive. They trick our bodies into copying them until there is enough virus to be dangerous.

Red blood cells infected with the *Plasmodium* protist, which causes malaria

Yersinia pestis bacterium (causes bubonic plague)

Variola virus (causes smallpox)

FLU VIRUS

NOW THAT'S SMALL! How big are germs? In the width of one human hair, you could fit 200 protists such as Plasmodium. The same space would fit 500 bubonic plague bacteria or 3,300 Variola viruses. No wonder they went unnoticed for so long!

RABIES

GERMS

Not all germs spread diseases. Some do useful things, such as turning dead plants into soil.

UNDER THE MICROSCOPE

A germ is our tiniest enemy. No matter how closely you look, you will not see one. But in the 17th century, a new invention – the microscope – suddenly gave scientists a clear view of small objects. Its magnifying lenses at last enabled them to spot the pesky blighters that make us ill. Microscopes are still used in laboratories, but they do not solve every health problem. Knowing what a germ looks like is often no help in stopping the disease it causes.

BRING 'EM CLOSER!

Laboratory microscopes work by magnifying in two stages. An 'objective' lens near the bottom forms an enlarged picture of whatever is right underneath it. Then an 'eyepiece' lens at the top of the microscope magnifies the picture again. Together, the two lenses can make things look 2,000 times larger than they really are. That is easily enough to see bacteria and protists very clearly.

BIGGER BACTERIA

You cannot avoid bacteria. A teaspoon of soil contains 200 million. Fortunately, only a few cause infection (spread disease). You can see individual bacteria with a microscope that magnifies only 100 times. Bacteria breed fast, forming vast colonies (groups). Look out for them as coloured spots on rotting food.

INVENTING THE FIRST MICROSCOPE

The first person to look at a germ was a Dutch cloth merchant called Anton van Leeuwenhoek (left). He did it using microscopes the size of his thumb. They had tiny glass beads for lenses. In around 1675, he used his microscopes to study first protists, then bacteria. He called these tiny creatures 'animalcules' (little animals), but never guessed they caused disease.

A CLOSER LOOK AT PROTISTS

You will find protists anywhere wet. A bit bigger than bacteria, they are easy to see with a microscope. Some, such as algae (left), feed on light as plants do. Others are more like animals, and wiggle around searching for food. Protists that live in our bodies as part of their life-cycle can make us very ill. Plasmodium, for instance, causes malaria.

Green algae

MAGNIFYING VIRUSES

Viruses are so small that it takes a powerful electron microscope to show them up. They are not alive. To reproduce, they invade tiny body cells – the 'building blocks' of all living things. Once inside, a virus forces the cell itself to make more and more identical viruses. This damages the cell, causing disease. Viruses cannot be controlled by the antibiotic drugs that kill bacteria.

An electron microscope image of influenza virus particles

Ordinary microscopes use light to form enlarged pictures. But viruses are smaller than the smallest light beam, so they look fuzzy. To see them clearly, scientists point a beam of electrons – tiny particles – at the virus. An electron beam is 100,000 times finer than a light beam, and an electron microscope magnifies up to two million times. A scanning electron microscope (SEM) such as this one (right) sweeps the beam to-and-fro to make in-depth pictures.

DISEÂSE: HOW IT SPREADS

For you or me, infection (catching a disease) is bad news. It means discomfort, pain, or – if we're very, very unlucky – death. But for the germs that cause illness, infection means success! Each infected person multiplies the number of germs, and (unless they take care) spreads the disease. Most germs are much less extreme than this pair invading the Pox Lab. Germs don't usually lurk, or kill instantly. Instead, they cause obvious symptoms (signs of disease) and leave their victims just well enough to infect others.

THE SPY GERM

A sneaky way for a germ to survive and thrive is to hide in a victim's body and cause no obvious symptoms – at first. The infected person lives a normal life, and slowly spreads the infection to others. Leprosy bacteria (see page 18) take this stealthy, spy-like approach. Sufferers can spread the disease on their breath for up to 20 years before the first signs of leprosy appear on their own skin.

PASSING IT ON

Diseases spread themselves around in clever ways. Some simply hitch a ride on a cough, a sneeze, or on unwashed hands. But a few are smarter. They move through the guts or blood of several creatures during different parts of their lives — for example, as one animal consumes another. Here are some common ways to catch disease:

BY MOUTH: infections enter our guts on food or drink, or dirty hands.

IN BLOOD: diseases in blood spread though open wounds or shared syringes.

FROM ANIMALS: living things such as lice, fleas or flies can pass on infections.

FROM OBJECTS: germs linger on things we handle, such as door knobs, coins or bank notes.

FROM DROPLETS: sick people infect others by coughing, sneezing or breathing.

THROUGH SEX: some diseases cause infection through sexual contact. This does **NOT** mean through normal, everyday contact such as touching or kissing.

THE WARRIOR GERM

Other infections are more warlike than stealthy. They have dramatic, often scary, symptoms. The symptoms spread the disease very quickly. Cholera bacteria work like this (see page 22). Someone swallowing them soon suffers from terrible sickness and diarrhoea. Each day, 10 to 20 litres of clear, watery liquid spills from their guts. The liquid contains millions of cholera bacteria. Cholera spreads quickly if the liquid pollutes drinking water.

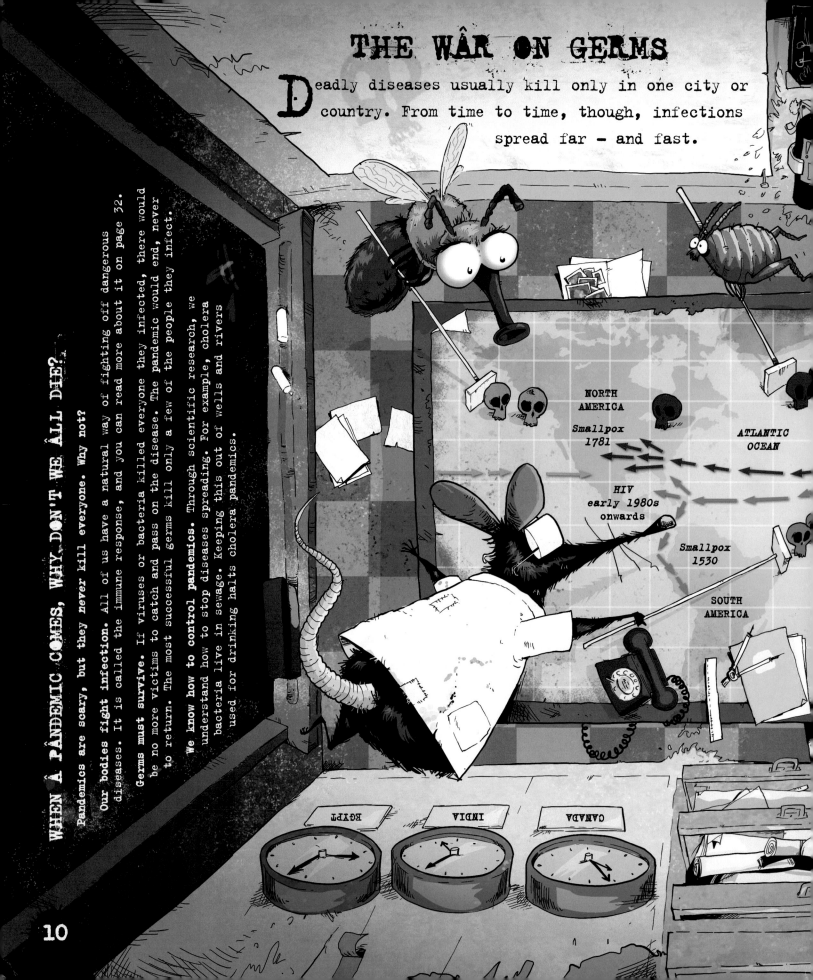

THE WÂR ON GERMS

Deadly diseases usually kill only in one city or country. From time to time, though, infections spread far – and fast.

WHEN A PÂNDEMIC COMES, WHY DON'T WE ÂLL DIE?

Pandemics are scary, but they never kill everyone. Why not?

Our bodies fight infection. All of us have a natural way of fighting off dangerous diseases. It is called the immune response, and you can read more about it on page 32.

Germs must survive. If viruses or bacteria killed everyone they infected, there would be no more victims to catch and pass on the disease. The pandemic would end, never to return. The most successful germs kill only a few of the people they infect.

We know how to control pandemics. Through scientific research, we understand how to stop diseases spreading. For example, cholera bacteria live in sewage. Keeping this out of wells and rivers used for drinking halts cholera pandemics.

NORTH AMERICA

Smallpox 1781

ATLANTIC OCEAN

HIV early 1980s onwards

Smallpox 1530

SOUTH AMERICA

EGYPT

INDIA

CANADA

The most serious infections become pandemics, outbreaks of disease that make people ill on several continents or even worldwide. The worst pandemics can kill millions.

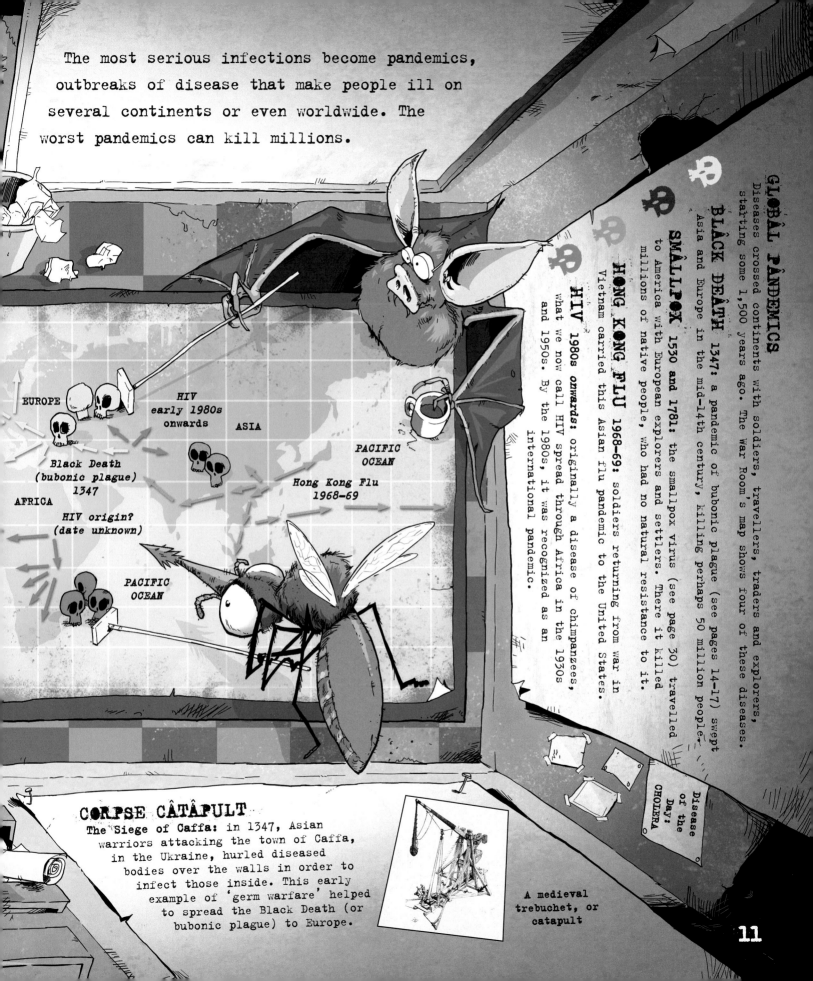

EUROPE

HIV
early 1980s
onwards

ASIA

PACIFIC
OCEAN

Black Death
(bubonic plague)
1347

Hong Kong Flu
1968–69

AFRICA

HIV origin?
(date unknown)

PACIFIC
OCEAN

GLOBAL PANDEMICS

Diseases crossed continents with soldiers, travellers, traders and explorers, starting some 1,500 years ago. The War Room's map shows four of these diseases.

BLACK DEATH 1347: a pandemic of bubonic plague (see pages 14–17) swept Asia and Europe in the mid-14th century, killing perhaps 50 million people.

SMALLPOX 1530 and 1781: the smallpox virus (see page 30) travelled to America with European explorers and settlers. There it killed millions of native people, who had no natural resistance to it.

HONG KONG FLU 1968–69: soldiers returning from war in Vietnam carried this Asian flu pandemic to the United States.

HIV 1980s *onwards*: originally a disease of chimpanzees, what we now call HIV spread through Africa in the 1930s and 1950s. By the 1980s, it was recognized as an international pandemic.

Disease
of the
Day:
CHOLERA

CORPSE CATAPULT

The Siege of Caffa: in 1347, Asian warriors attacking the town of Caffa, in the Ukraine, hurled diseased bodies over the walls in order to infect those inside. This early example of 'germ warfare' helped to spread the Black Death (or bubonic plague) to Europe.

A medieval
trebuchet, or
catapult

11

TYPHUS

Infection: bacteria, spread by the bite of a louse.
This used to be called ship or gaol fever because it spread quickly in crowded, dirty places. An epidemic in the 30 Years' War (1618-48) killed perhaps a third of Germans, ten times more than died in the fighting. It is now cured with antibiotics.

YELLOW FEVER

Infection: a virus, spread by a mosquito bite.
Named for the skin colour change it causes, yellow fever is a frightening disease. Victims bleed out of every opening in their body. There is no cure, but a vaccine protects against it. A terrible 1878 epidemic in southern USA killed 20,000 people.

TYPHOID

Infection: bacteria, spread by sewage in food or water.
Typhoid is still a major killer. It affects 17 million people every year, resulting in about 600,000 deaths — but clean water and soap can help to stop its spread. Victims have a fever and diarrhoea. Antibiotics and a simple sugar-and-salt drink can cure these symptoms.

THE ROGUES' GALLERY

There just isn't enough room in the Pox Lab to study all the nasty diseases that threaten human life. You can take a closer look at some of the worst offenders on the following pages. Portraits of the rest hang in this corridor. Our Rogues' Gallery is a reminder that disease comes in many disguises.

☞ **DENGUE FEVER**

Infection: a virus, spread by mosquito bites.

There is no way to prevent or cure this disease, which threatens two-fifths of the world's people. Sufferers have pain in their joints, which gives the disease its nickname, 'breakbone fever'. They are treated with painkillers and sweet drinks.

☞ **POLIO**

Infection: a virus, spread by sewage in food or water.

Polio infects young children, withering their muscles. Ancient Egyptian paintings (3,400 years old) show signs of the disease, but epidemics began only in the 20th century. In 1952, 3,500 Americans died of it. Vaccination now protects children from polio.

☞ **SLEEPING SICKNESS**

Infection: a protist, spread by a tsetse fly bite.

Explorers spread this one through 19th-century Africa. A 20-year epidemic in Uganda began in 1901, killing 250,000 people in total. Untreated, it kills as the protists invade the brain. Drug treatment is hard, but fly control is helping to stop the disease.

☞ **HIV**

Infection: a virus (right), spread by sexual contact or through infected blood (e.g. from using contaminated needles).

Short for human immunodeficiency virus, HIV stops the patient's body from fighting off other deadly infections. Though drug treatments can control HIV, it still kills about two million people every year, mostly in Africa. However, in countries where the right kind of medical care is available, people can live for many years with HIV.

Physicians were as scared as anyone. To protect themselves from infection, many wore beaked masks, and used a stick to prod and poke sufferers. The 'cures' they offered did not help, and often harmed those who took them.

1. Healthy rat

2. Infected flea bites rat

3. Rat dies

4. Fleas flee to human

5. Flea bites human

6. Rest in peace

SPREADING THE PLAGUE

It was not the rats themselves that spread the Black Death; it was the fleas that lived on them. The fleas caught the disease from infected rats, and spread it by biting healthy rats. When these rats died of the disease, the fleas hopped onto people... and passed it to them, too. In a cruel twist, killing the rats just made the problem worse. Fleas need living homes, so they fled the horrid, cold rat corpses for nice, warm, living human bodies.

BLÂCK DEÂTH

Rats. Sleek and clever, they scampered everywhere in 14th-century towns. They gobbled food and left trails of filth. But in 1347 rats also spread a deadly disease. Nicknamed the 'Black Death' after the horrible swellings on victims' bodies, the bubonic plague killed more than a third of all European people. Terrified survivors did not know that rats caused the disease. Instead, they blamed bad behaviour, bad smells – even tight clothes!

...AND HOW TO STOP IT

Panicking city governments tried everything they could think of to stop the plague. One of them succeeded. It was in Dubrovnik, a Croatian city then ruled by Venice. In 1397, the city council made all arriving visitors stay on a nearby island. Only those still healthy after 30 days (the period later rose to 40 days) were let into the city. This time of closely-watched separation was called quarantine, after the Italian words *quaranta giorni* ('40 days').

HOW TO SPOT IT...

The frightening signs of the Black Death appeared within two and ten days of a flea bite. Some victims first got terrible headaches and backaches, and were confused. But everyone who was infected suffered a sudden high fever. If a smooth swelling, called a bubo, appeared in the neck, armpits or groin, a painful death was just days away. Other signs included coughing and vomiting blood.

THE SEARCH FOR A CURE

Rich plague sufferers swallowed useless drinks made mostly from plants and trees: dittany, pimpernel, tormentil, roses, violets, fumitory, myrrh and crocus. If these did not work, a doctor opened the patient's veins to let the blood run out – a treatment that was sometimes deadlier than the disease itself. The poor could only pray they would escape death. Priests urged them to avoid luxury, hot baths, fruit and rude behaviour. Often, those who obeyed these rules died anyway.

15

THE PLAGUE SPREADS!

The Black Death, or bubonic plague, crossed continents like a murderous passenger, hitching a lift with infected rats, fleas and people. It reached southeast Europe in 1347. By autumn the next year, it was killing people in Britain. Fear helped to spread the disease. Whenever it reached a new town, terrified citizens tried to escape. Many were already infected, though they seemed healthy. They carried the disease onwards to the next town... and the next...

STARVATION followed the plague, because the disease killed workers who grew food plants, and stopped trade in grain. However, surviving farm workers were better off when the Black Death was over. There were fewer of them, so they demanded – and got – higher wages.

FLEEING by road or in crowded ships was a luxury only the rich could afford. Travel was expensive, and poor people could not leave their land and homes.

HOW MANY GRAVES?

Experts calculate that the 14th-century outbreak of Black Death killed up to 50 million people in Europe and Asia. More died in later epidemics.

THE SPREAD OF THE BUBONIC PLAGUE (BLACK DEATH)

AREAS AFFECTED BY 1347

AREAS AFFECTED BY 1348

AREAS AFFECTED BY 1349

AREAS AFFECTED BY 1350–52, OR NOT AT ALL

1350

1349

NORTH SEA

1349

1348

London

1349

Cologne

1349

1348

Paris

Mains

Strasbourg

1349

ATLANTIC OCEAN

1348–49

Lyon

1348

Bordeaux

1348

Genoa

Toulouse

Marseilles

Aix

1347

1347

1349

1348

Barcelona

1348

Toledo

1348

1348

Valencia

1348

1347

MEDITERRANEAN SEA

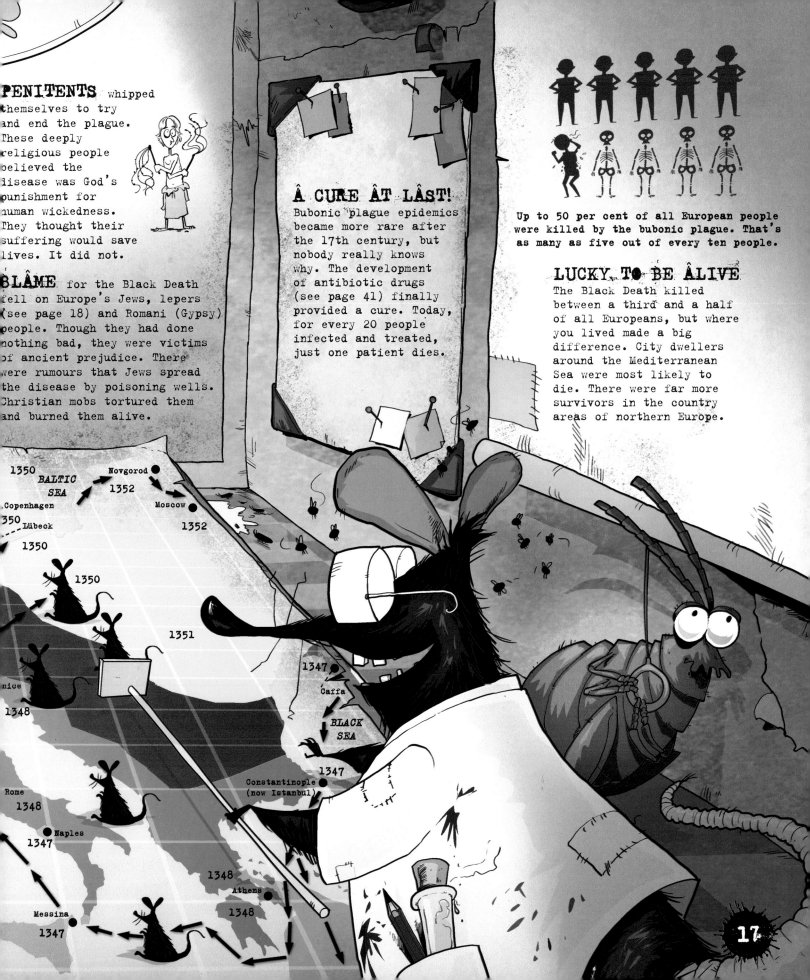

PENITENTS whipped themselves to try and end the plague. These deeply religious people believed the disease was God's punishment for human wickedness. They thought their suffering would save lives. It did not.

BLAME for the Black Death fell on Europe's Jews, lepers (see page 18) and Romani (Gypsy) people. Though they had done nothing bad, they were victims of ancient prejudice. There were rumours that Jews spread the disease by poisoning wells. Christian mobs tortured them and burned them alive.

A CURE AT LAST!
Bubonic plague epidemics became more rare after the 17th century, but nobody really knows why. The development of antibiotic drugs (see page 41) finally provided a cure. Today, for every 20 people infected and treated, just one patient dies.

Up to 50 per cent of all European people were killed by the bubonic plague. That's as many as five out of every ten people.

LUCKY TO BE ALIVE
The Black Death killed between a third and a half of all Europeans, but where you lived made a big difference. City dwellers around the Mediterranean Sea were most likely to die. There were far more survivors in the country areas of northern Europe.

1350
BALTIC SEA
Novgorod
1352
Copenhagen
1350 Lübeck
1350
Moscow
1352
1350
1351
nice
1348
Rome
1348
Naples
1348
Messina
1347
1347
Caffa
BLACK SEA
1347
Constantinople (now Istanbul)
1348
Athens
1348

Leprosy began in eastern Africa, but it was spread across the world by trade and slavery. Migration carried the disease into Europe and Asia. It crossed the Atlantic Ocean to the Caribbean islands and Brazil on 17th-century slave ships. Lepers were among the West African people captured by European merchants and transported to South America to work as slaves.

Medieval priests used Bible stories to convince people that leprosy was God's punishment for evil.

NORTH AMERICA

EUROPE

ASIA

Caribbean Sea

ATLANTIC OCEAN

West Africa

SOUTH AMERICA

Brazil

"UNCLEÂN, UNCLEÂN!"

In a medieval street, a hooded beggar hobbles slowly along. He rings a bell and croaks "Unclean!" to warn that he is coming. Children stare at his damaged face and missing fingers. Kindly adults leave food for him, but shrink from his touch. They worry they will catch his disease, leprosy, and that they too will become an outcast leper like him.

ÂN ÂNCIENT DISEÂSE

Stories from the Bible and from ancient Greece and Rome, 3,000 years ago, describe a disease much like leprosy, and tell how lepers were badly treated. The oldest physical evidence of leprosy is from Jerusalem, from the time of Jesus Christ. In 2009, archaeologists digging in the Hinnom Valley found leprosy bacteria in the body of a man buried in a cave there some 2,000 years ago.

The leper's tomb, near Jerusalem in the Holy Land, was well preserved because the entrance was sealed.

THE DREADED LEPER

Fear and ignorance kept lepers apart from society. Research has shown that leprosy (or Hansen's disease) is not a danger to 19 in every 20 people. Modern drugs easily cure it. But eight centuries ago, leprosy was a frightening mystery. Lepers were locked up together in colonies. They had to wear special marks, such as yellow crosses, and they had to keep well away from other people.

Lepers shook a warning bell or wooden clapper.

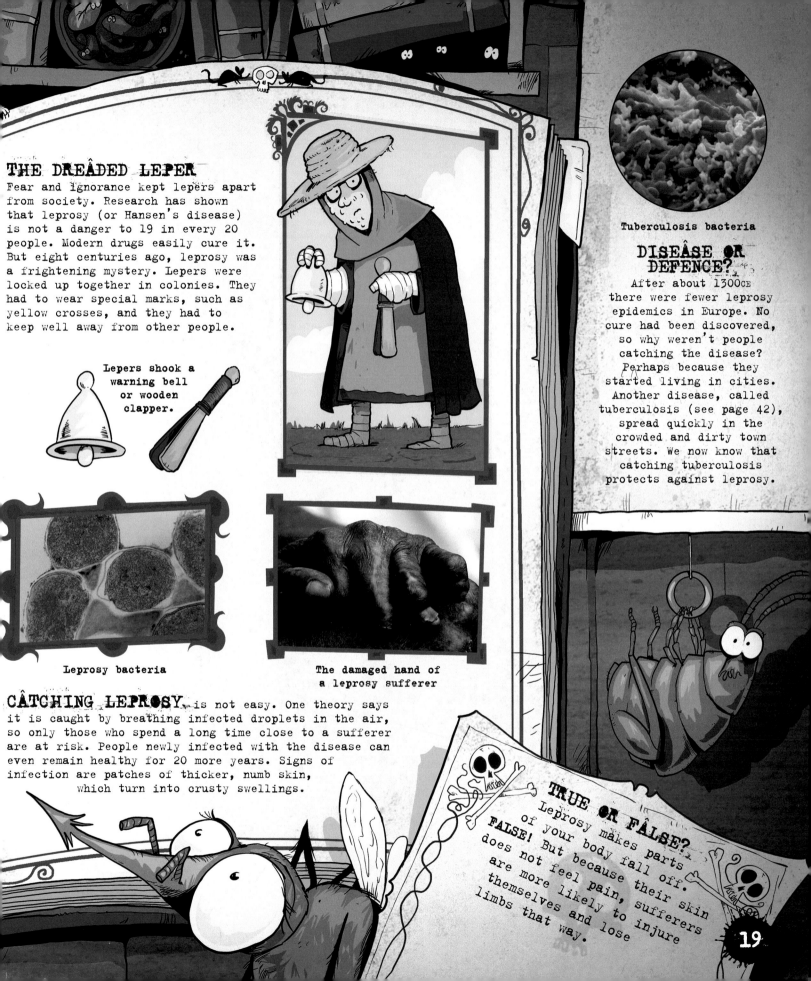

Tuberculosis bacteria

DISEÂSE OR DEFENCE?

After about 1300CE there were fewer leprosy epidemics in Europe. No cure had been discovered, so why weren't people catching the disease? Perhaps because they started living in cities. Another disease, called tuberculosis (see page 42), spread quickly in the crowded and dirty town streets. We now know that catching tuberculosis protects against leprosy.

Leprosy bacteria

The damaged hand of a leprosy sufferer

CÂTCHING LEPROSY is not easy. One theory says

it is caught by breathing infected droplets in the air, so only those who spend a long time close to a sufferer are at risk. People newly infected with the disease can even remain healthy for 20 more years. Signs of infection are patches of thicker, numb skin, which turn into crusty swellings.

TRUE OR FÂLSE?

Leprosy makes parts of your body fall off. **FALSE!** But because their skin does not feel pain, sufferers are more likely to injure themselves and lose limbs that way.

19

A DEADLY DEBATE

Two centuries ago, doctors argued about the causes of disease. They practised what they believed – but often their 'treatments' were worthless, or made patients more ill. Common ideas on how people got sick were centuries old – and mostly wrong. And without scientific explanations of how diseases spread, doctors could do little to stop them. Here are some of their ideas...

THE HUMOURS

The *Theory of Humours* sounds like a joke, but doctors had taken it seriously since around 400BCE. Humours (they believed) were four liquids that filled human bodies: blood, phlegm (snot), yellow bile and black bile. For good health the four humours had to be in balance. If they were not, sickness was the result. It seemed like a good idea – for blood, phlegm and bile do spill from sick people – but the *Theory of Humours* was also completely *wrong*.

In this cartoon (left), a miasma is rampaging through 19th-century London, causing a cholera epidemic.

MIASMA

Doctors had known since the first century CE that people became ill near swamps, sewers, and piles of filth or manure... in fact, almost anywhere that smelt bad. They thought that 'harmful, poisonous gases called 'miasmas' spread from these places. This theory fitted the facts, but it was wrong.

BLOOD: air,
spring

PHLEGM:
water,
winter

YELLOW
BILE:
fire,
summer

BLACK BILE:
earth, autumn

Each of the humours was
linked to a season and to
one of the elements – the
four kinds of matter from
which everything was made,
according to ancient people.

SIN

Religious leaders taught that
illness was God's punishment
for sin (evil or ungodly acts
and thoughts). Epidemics made
this idea hard to believe.
They cruelly killed countless
good and deeply religious
people, but sometimes spared
the lives of the
wicked and
godless.

CONTÂGION

Arab scholars had suggested in the
14th century CE that sickness might
begin when 'minute bodies' invaded
a healthy person. A century later,
Italian physician Fracastorius
agreed. He blamed 'disease seeds'
for causing infection, and thought
that sick people could pass them
on to others through infected
objects such as clothes.
His ideas were similar
to modern germ theory,
but at the time doctors
laughed at these
new proposals.

THE MEDICÂL DETECTIVE

Most 'experts' thought that a miasma (see page 20) or the touch of a victim caused cholera. But physician John Snow did not agree. He was sure polluted water was the source. Snow was a respected doctor. He was also a pioneer of anaesthetics — drugs that make patients sleep through painful surgery. His ideas about the spread of cholera were unusual, and many doctors laughed at them. Snow talked to ordinary people in Soho, a London neighbourhood badly hit by this new epidemic. The terrified slum-dwellers there told him how many people had died, and where they had lived. Snow plotted the deaths on a map (far right). His map proved that water was indeed to blame. It also suggested how he could halt the spread of cholera.

Many families in Soho shared a single privy (lavatory). It was often no more than a hole in the ground, with a seat above it.

Â HÂND PUMP drew water from the well in Broad Street. Snow took off the pump handle, forcing everyone to drink clean water from other wells. Almost immediately, the Soho epidemic ended. It might have stopped anyway, but Snow's hunch was right. Cholera spread when a victim used a privy, and sewage from it seeped into an underground well.

THE UNWELL WELL

Bad smells were always part of London life, but in 1854 the stink was worse than usual. An epidemic of deadly cholera — the world's worst stomach upset — gripped the city. Sufferers' guts emptied so quickly into the overflowing privies that their bodies dried out and shrivelled. The disease was killing thousands, but what was causing it?

John Snow (1813-58) gave England's Queen Victoria anaesthetics to ease her pain when she gave birth.

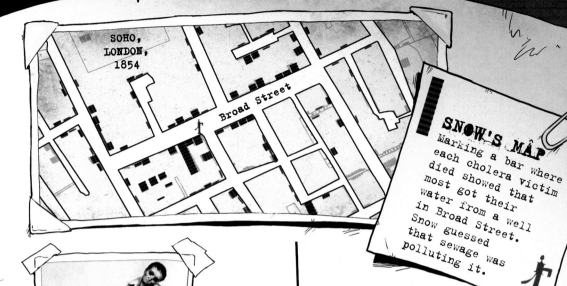

SOHO, LONDON, 1854

Broad Street

SNOW'S MAP
Marking a bar where each cholera victim died showed that most got their water from a well in Broad Street. Snow guessed that sewage was polluting it.

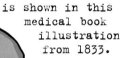

SUDDEN FEVER

A bad stomach ache and violent, watery diarrhoea were the signs of cholera. Loss of fluid dried out victims' bodies, shrinking them and turning their skin blue – as is shown in this medical book illustration from 1833.

NEW SEWERS

Doctors and politicians eventually accepted Snow's ideas. In 1859, construction began on a system of sewers for London. These huge pipes collected human waste from privies and carried it safely away. After the completion of these sewers, and fresh water pipes, the city never again suffered from a cholera epidemic.

This drawing, from the time of the epidemic, shows the ghostly figure of Death drawing water from the Broad Street pump.

This photograph shows the construction of the London sewerage system in 1859.

BUG BREAKTHROUGH

Doctors could not stop epidemic diseases until science began to make giant steps forward in the 19th century. Real research started with the work of three great scientists: Louis Pasteur, Robert Koch and Ferdinand Cohn. Together, they proved that germs spread disease – and found ways to prevent them spreading.

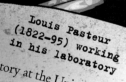

Louis Pasteur (1822–95) working in his laboratory

In his laboratory at the University of Lille, France, biologist Louis Pasteur tried to find out why wine and beer sometimes became sour and undrinkable. Pasteur showed that these drinks soured when microbes (germs) from the air drifted into them. By gently heating the beer and wine, Pasteur killed off the microbes and preserved the drinks for longer. Heating cow's milk in the same way preserved that, too. Pasteur's germ-killing heat treatment was named after him: 'Pasteurization'.

Germ Theory

Pasteur also observed broth (meat soup) going bad. To prove that it was microbes drifting in the air that turned the soup bad, he tried keeping them out. He heated two samples of broth to kill off the microbes. He left one sample open to the air. Microbes settled, and mould grew on it. The other sample he kept in a flask with a curving neck. The U-shaped glass bend trapped the microbes, and nothing grew on the broth inside.

SÂFER MILK

Robert Koch found tuberculosis (TB) in cows' milk, but he was not sure that it could cause TB in humans. Once we knew we could get TB from contaminated milk, pasteurization equipment was installed in many farms and factories (above). Now, shops sell only pasteurized milk.

Robert Koch
(1843–1910)

Ferdinand Cohn
(1828–98)

MICROBE HUNTERS

While Pasteur worked in France, two German scientists were also studying microbes. Ferdinand Cohn named the different types of bacteria. He showed that some turned into seed-like spores to survive harsh conditions. Robert Koch went further. He identified the bacteria that caused anthrax, tuberculosis and cholera infections. Tuberculosis alone killed up to a third of 19th-century city-dwellers. Koch's brilliant work led eventually to a vaccine (see page 43) to protect against the disease.

Together with Koch and Cohn, Pasteur helped to launch the science of microbiology: the study of living things too small to see with the naked eye.

DEATH IN THE AIR

On a summer's walk, they are just a pesky irritation. In a quiet bedroom, their annoying buzz makes sleep impossible. But in hot, wet countries, mosquitoes can mean deadly peril. For the bites of these tiny, flying insects spread a dangerous disease called malaria. Sufferers have a fever that makes them hot and sweaty one minute, then teeth-chatteringly cold the next. The fever returns every two days. Without treatment, malaria causes damage to the blood that can kill a victim.

1. Mosquito is infected

5. New mozzy takes infected red blood cells from the victim

LIFE OF A KILLER

The cause of malaria is a protist, called *Plasmodium*. When a mosquito feeds on a malaria sufferer, it sucks up *Plasmodium* with the blood it drinks. The protist thrives inside the mosquito. When the insect bites again, the protist is injected into the victim's blood. In the human body, *Plasmodium* hides and multiplies in the liver and blood. Damaged blood cells stick together, causing deadly blockages in arteries (blood pipes).

2. Parasites spread in mozzy's gut

4. Parasites move to the human liver

3. Infection injected into a human

SWAMPS AND MARSHES

People once called malaria 'swamp fever' because there were more sufferers near marshland. Ignoring the insects breeding in the smelly water, they thought that bad vapours rising from the swamps caused malaria. The disease's modern name comes from Italian words meaning 'evil air'.

EARLY REMEDIES

In 17th-century Peru, malaria sufferers chewed the bark of a shrub they called 'the fever tree'. It is known today as Cinchona, and the healing chemical in the bark is called quinine. Chinese healers used to treat malaria with a herb called sweet wormwood. An extract from it is the source of a modern drug called Artemisinin.

MODERN REMEDIES

Malaria is still a huge problem in Africa, South Asia and South America, but preventing it is simple. Mosquitoes feed at night, so covering beds in insecticide-soaked nets stops them from biting. Sadly, the people most at risk of malaria are too poor to buy the nets, and a million die each year. Most are children younger than five years old. Spraying insecticide on stagnant pools helps to stop mosquitoes from breeding, and there are drug cures such as Artemisinin. These are costly, but they work well.

Mosquito nets over beds

Spraying an insecticide

Malaria spread through Europe, c. 500-1500CE.

In ancient times, migrating people spread malaria to the Middle East and Asia.

NORTH AMERICA

EUROPE

Greece, c. 300BCE

ASIA

China, c. 2700BCE

Italy, c. 200BCE

northern India, c. 1000BCE

Atlantic Ocean

Egypt, c. 1500BCE

AFRICA

SOUTH AMERICA

More than 30 million years ago, malaria parasites infected apes and ancient humans.

European explorers carried malaria to North and South America from c. 1500CE.

WORLDWIDE EXPANSION

Malaria leaves no marks on skeletons, so scientists are unable to trace its spread by studying old human remains. However, it is impossible to confuse malaria with other diseases. Throughout history, writers have described its symptoms, and through their stories we can follow malaria's deadly path (see above). It probably started in Africa, spread east through China and India; then north to Europe; and finally, westwards to America.

THE RESISTANCE

In 2009, treatment given to malaria sufferers in Thailand and Cambodia failed to cure them. The *Plasmodium* protists in their blood had developed a resistance to Artemisinin and other drugs. Health officials rushed to the region to try and wipe out this new, more dangerous form of the disease. For if this resistance spreads, there will no longer be a cure for malaria.

CHILDHOOD DISEÂSES

In the slums of 19th-century cities, children could not hide from death's bony hand. For disease spread quickly among the hungry kids who lived in filthy homes. As many as one in three did not live long enough to celebrate their first birthday. Cities remained deadly places until there was better housing, and until vaccines reduced child deaths in the 20th century.

CROWDED CITIES

Poor families could not afford to rent a whole house or apartment, so many shared a single room with another family – or even two more. In New York City, USA, the most crowded homes were in 'tenements'. These tall buildings were split into dozens of tiny rooms, most without windows, running water or lavatories. Disease raced through them in the summer: in New York alone, more than 100 children died each day in July 1876.

Â DISEÂSE OF DEÂDLY SPOTS

In the case of some childhood diseases, the germs that cause them are always lurking, waiting for a chance to strike. Measles, for instance, infects almost everyone who shares a room with a sufferer. It is passed on in the air they breathe out, and in slime from their nose and mouth. It once killed a quarter of all the slum children who caught it. Those who survived became immune (they could not catch it again). The measles virus needs 250,000 non-immune people for it to spread, so measles outbreaks ended naturally, only to return when immunity levels fell.

A child-sized coffin – a much more common sight in the 19th century

The skin rash caused by measles

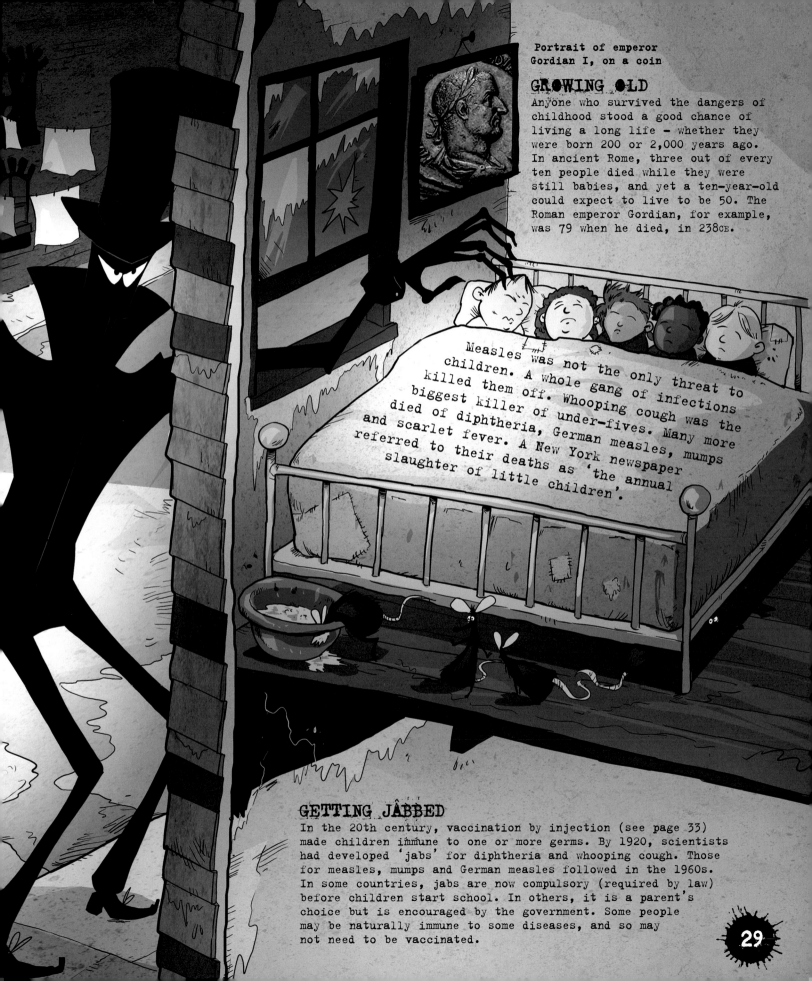

Portrait of emperor
Gordian I, on a coin

GROWING OLD

Anyone who survived the dangers of
childhood stood a good chance of
living a long life — whether they
were born 200 or 2,000 years ago.
In ancient Rome, three out of every
ten people died while they were
still babies, and yet a ten-year-old
could expect to live to be 50. The
Roman emperor Gordian, for example,
was 79 when he died, in 238CE.

Measles was not the only threat to
children. A whole gang of infections
killed them off. Whooping cough was the
biggest killer of under-fives. Many more
died of diphtheria, German measles, mumps
and scarlet fever. A New York newspaper
referred to their deaths as 'the annual
slaughter of little children'.

GETTING JÂBBED

In the 20th century, vaccination by injection (see page 33)
made children immune to one or more germs. By 1920, scientists
had developed 'jabs' for diphtheria and whooping cough. Those
for measles, mumps and German measles followed in the 1960s.
In some countries, jabs are now compulsory (required by law)
before children start school. In others, it is a parent's
choice but is encouraged by the government. Some people
may be naturally immune to some diseases, and so may
not need to be vaccinated.

29

CURING THE POX

In the stuffy darkness of an Egyptian tomb, archaeologists prize open a stone coffin, and gaze at the face of a long-dead pharaoh. Then they jump back in alarm, for blisters cover the face of the king! There is no mistaking this rash... the pharaoh died of smallpox! This deadly disease claimed millions of lives around the world, until a vaccine wiped it out by 1980.

The 12th-century BCE pharaoh Ramesses V died of smallpox.

Some who survive the disease have faces scarred for ever by blisters.

Smallpox blisters are so close together that some victims have blisters on their blisters!

THE BIRTH OF A DISEASE

Smallpox used to spread when large numbers of people lived close together. So scientists guess that the disease began when wandering people began to farm land and live in larger groups some 12,000 years ago. Smallpox probably started as an illness of farm animals in Africa or Asia. It may have infected humans when we began sheltering farm animals in our homes. By the time great civilizations grew up in Egypt, India, China and Greece, smallpox epidemics were already causing suffering and fear.

SMALLPOX EPIDEMICS

People infected with smallpox remained healthy for nearly two weeks after they caught it. In that time they may have travelled and spread the virus far and wide. In China, there were epidemics in the 4th century CE. The disease spread to Japan in the 730s. There it killed half a million people in just one city, Nara. A Persian doctor called Rhazes wrote about the disease in the 10th century, when smallpox was common in Europe, Asia and Africa. Smallpox epidemics in Europe were still killing 400,000 people, annually, 800 years later.

Bathing in a soothing mineral bath was thought to ease the suffering.

EXPORTING A KILLER

When Europeans crossed the Atlantic to America in the 16th century, they took smallpox with them. The native Americans they conquered (above) had no resistance to the virus. Millions died. In Mexico alone, it killed about a third of the country's people in just six months of 1520.

USELESS REMEDIES

There were many 'cures' for smallpox. Japanese sufferers bathed in a soup of rice wine, beans and salt. Brazilians rubbed horse dung on the blisters. Indians avoided fried and spicy food. European doctors preferred to drain the blood of smallpox patients. But the most popular treatment was a colour: red. People believed red blinds, red clothes and red hats would cure the disease. In fact, none of these treatments had any effect at all.

THE REAL CURE

The cure for smallpox turned out to be... smallpox itself! While epidemics raged across Europe, people in Africa and the Middle East already knew of a preventative treatment: non-sufferers would scratch their own skin, and then rub in pus drawn from a blister on the skin of a sufferer. This protection saved the lives of five out of every six children who later caught the disease. African slave Onesimus introduced this method of protection, called inoculation, to Americans in around 1713. English noblewoman Mary Wortley Montagu learned it in Turkey four years later.

A bronze statuette of Onesimus

Lady Mary Wortley Montagu

FIGHTING BACK

Pox and plague would have wiped us all out long ago if our bodies had no way to fight disease. Fortunately, each of us has a natural defence known as the immune system. This guards against infections and helps us to recover from them. Remarkably, our immune system has a memory. Like a warehouse filled with records of each illness we catch, this protects us from suffering a second dose. Immunization gives us a similar protection — without the danger of catching the first infection.

WHITE BLOOD CELLS

IMMUNE SYSTEM: ARCHIVE DEPT.

TOXINS

VIRAL INFECTIONS

PLAGUE BACTERIA

NATURAL IMMUNITY

Our skin is a visible barrier against germs, but most of the immune system is hidden in our blood. White cells in the blood recognize any germ, then surround it and kill it. But they also do more, in a defence called acquired immunity. When we catch a disease for the first time, the white cells produce chemicals called antibodies. An antibody fights off only the germ that causes the disease we have just caught. Antibodies stay in our blood, ready to defend us if the same type of germ attacks again.

UNKNOWN PATHOGENS

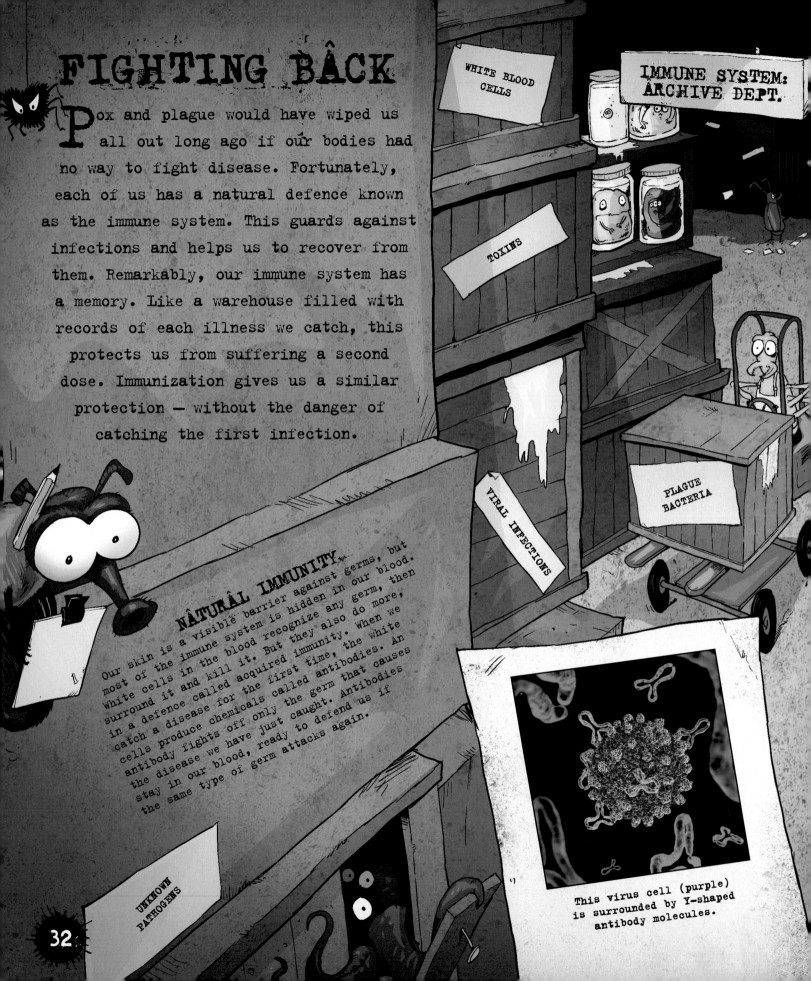

This virus cell (purple) is surrounded by Y-shaped antibody molecules.

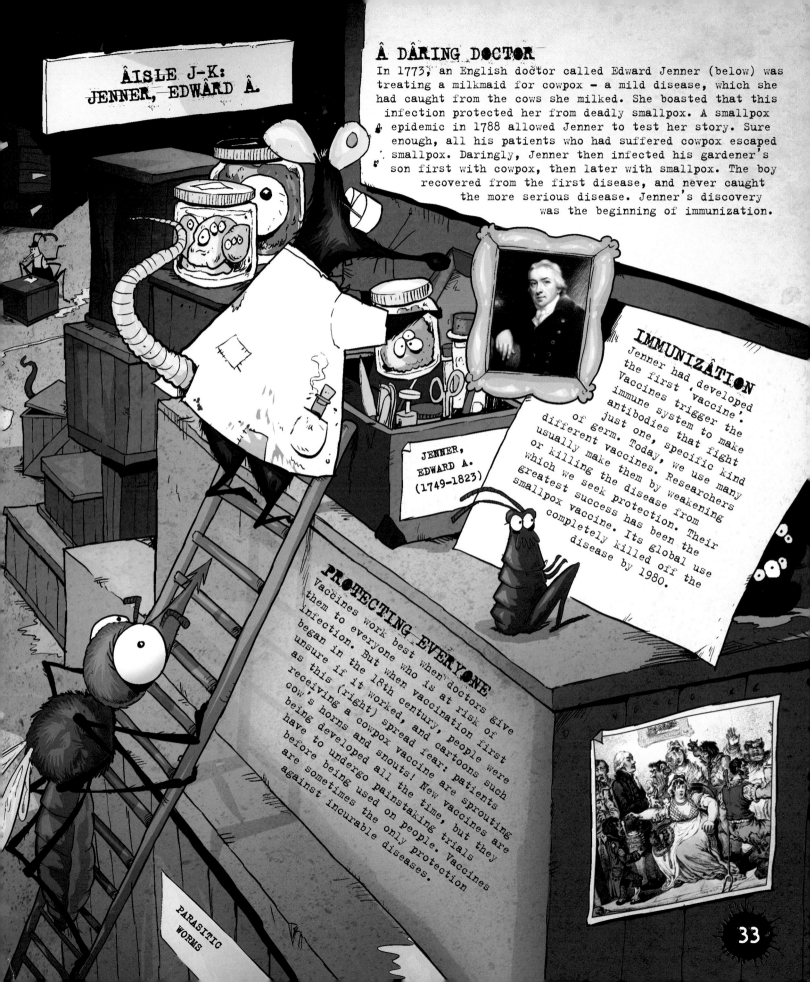

AISLE J-K: JENNER, EDWARD A.

A DARING DOCTOR

In 1773, an English doctor called Edward Jenner (below) was treating a milkmaid for cowpox — a mild disease, which she had caught from the cows she milked. She boasted that this infection protected her from deadly smallpox. A smallpox epidemic in 1788 allowed Jenner to test her story. Sure enough, all his patients who had suffered cowpox escaped smallpox. Daringly, Jenner then infected his gardener's son first with cowpox, then later with smallpox. The boy recovered from the first disease, and never caught the more serious disease. Jenner's discovery was the beginning of immunization.

JENNER,
EDWARD A.
(1749–1823)

IMMUNIZATION

Jenner had developed the first 'vaccine'. Vaccines trigger the immune system to make antibodies that fight just one, specific kind of germ. Today, we use many different vaccines. Researchers usually make them by weakening or killing the disease from which we seek protection. Their greatest success has been the smallpox vaccine. Its global use completely killed off the disease by 1980.

PROTECTING EVERYONE

Vaccines work best when doctors give them to everyone who is at risk of infection. But when vaccination first began in the 18th century, people were unsure if it worked, and cartoons such as this (right) spread fear: patients receiving a cowpox vaccine are sprouting cow's horns and snouts! New vaccines have to undergo all the time, but they being used on people. Vaccines are sometimes the only protection against incurable diseases.

PARASITIC
WORMS

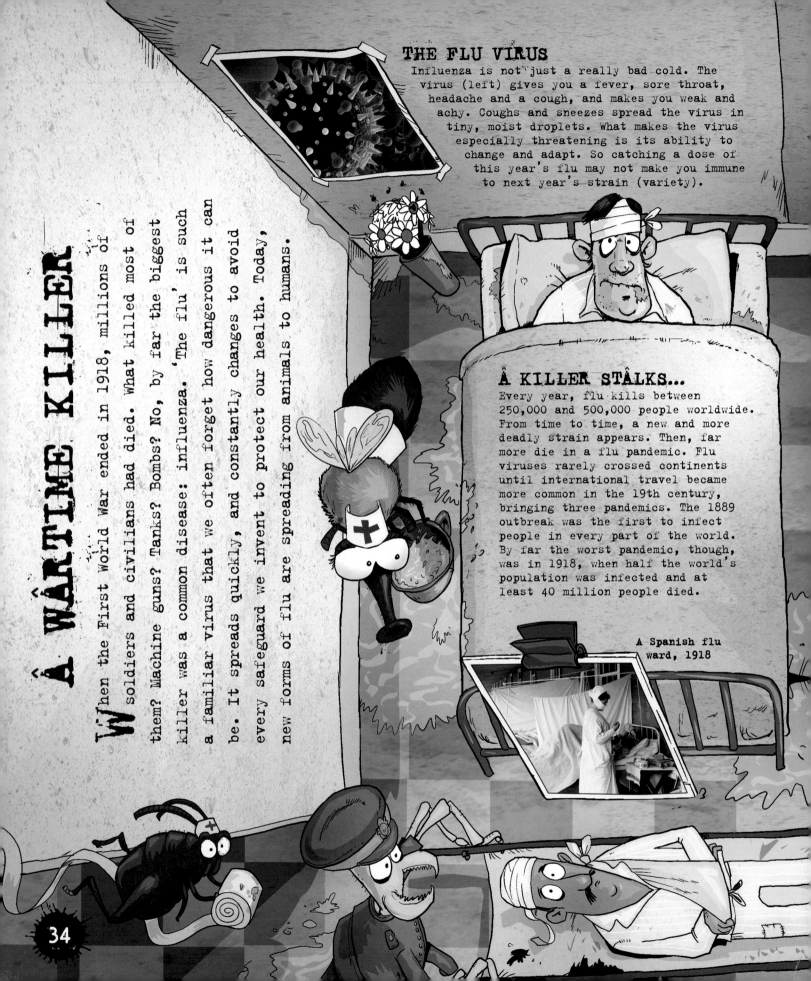

Â WÂRTIME KILLER

When the First World War ended in 1918, millions of soldiers and civilians had died. What killed most of them? Machine guns? Tanks? Bombs? No, by far the biggest killer was a common disease: influenza. 'The flu' is such a familiar virus that we often forget how dangerous it can be. It spreads quickly, and constantly changes to avoid every safeguard we invent to protect our health. Today, new forms of flu are spreading from animals to humans.

THE FLU VIRUS

Influenza is not just a really bad cold. The virus (left) gives you a fever, sore throat, headache and a cough, and makes you weak and achy. Coughs and sneezes spread the virus in tiny, moist droplets. What makes the virus especially threatening is its ability to change and adapt. So catching a dose of this year's flu may not make you immune to next year's strain (variety).

Â KILLER STÂLKS...

Every year, flu kills between 250,000 and 500,000 people worldwide. From time to time, a new and more deadly strain appears. Then, far more die in a flu pandemic. Flu viruses rarely crossed continents until international travel became more common in the 19th century, bringing three pandemics. The 1889 outbreak was the first to infect people in every part of the world. By far the worst pandemic, though, was in 1918, when half the world's population was infected and at least 40 million people died.

A Spanish flu ward, 1918

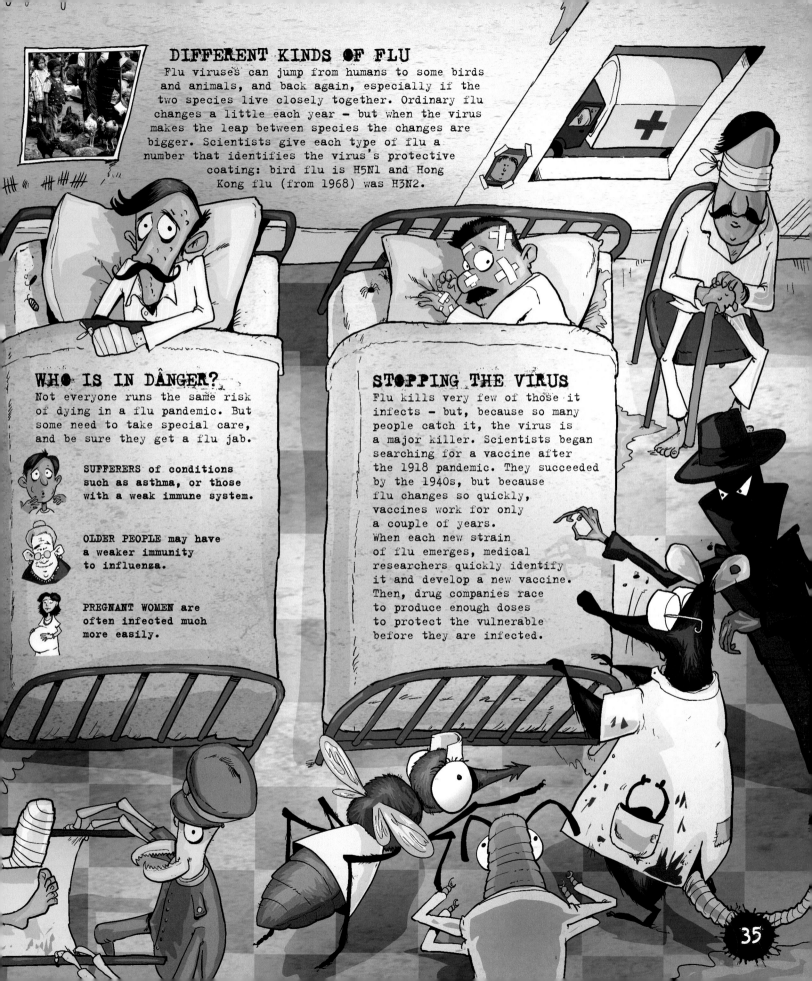

DIFFERENT KINDS OF FLU

Flu viruses can jump from humans to some birds and animals, and back again, especially if the two species live closely together. Ordinary flu changes a little each year — but when the virus makes the leap between species the changes are bigger. Scientists give each type of flu a number that identifies the virus's protective coating: bird flu is H5N1 and Hong Kong flu (from 1968) was H3N2.

WHO IS IN DANGER?

Not everyone runs the same risk of dying in a flu pandemic. But some need to take special care, and be sure they get a flu jab.

SUFFERERS of conditions such as asthma, or those with a weak immune system.

OLDER PEOPLE may have a weaker immunity to influenza.

PREGNANT WOMEN are often infected much more easily.

STOPPING THE VIRUS

Flu kills very few of those it infects — but, because so many people catch it, the virus is a major killer. Scientists began searching for a vaccine after the 1918 pandemic. They succeeded by the 1940s, but because flu changes so quickly, vaccines work for only a couple of years. When each new strain of flu emerges, medical researchers quickly identify it and develop a new vaccine. Then, drug companies race to produce enough doses to protect the vulnerable before they are infected.

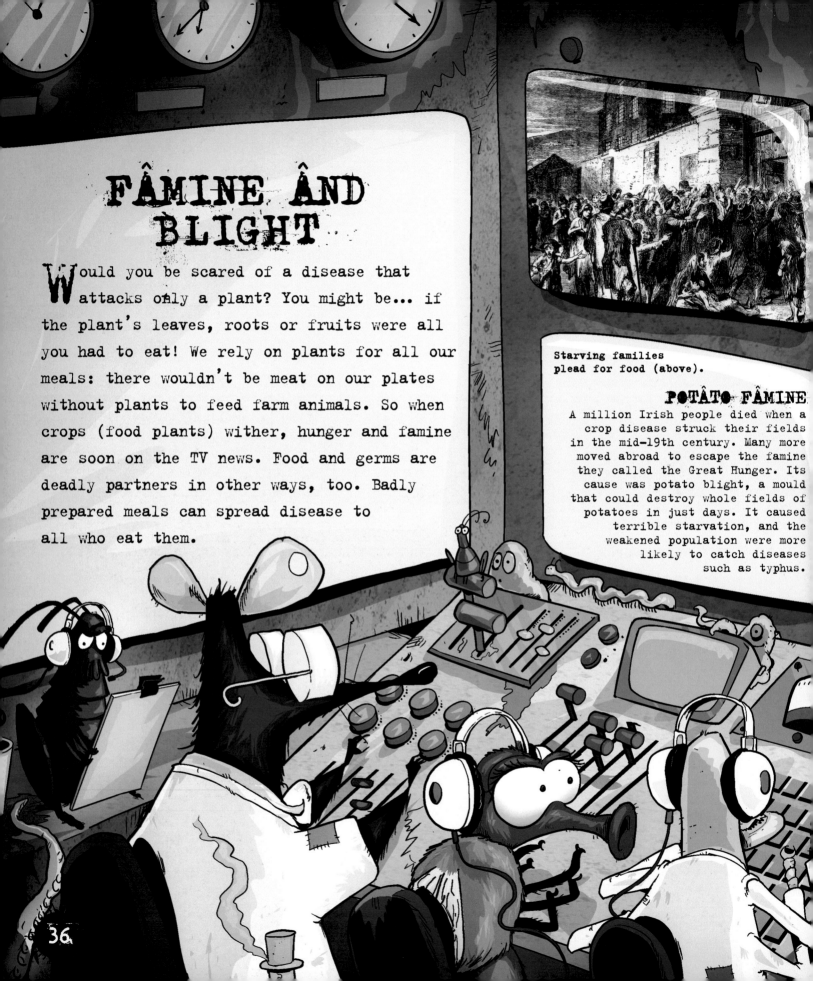

FÂMINE ÂND BLIGHT

Would you be scared of a disease that attacks only a plant? You might be... if the plant's leaves, roots or fruits were all you had to eat! We rely on plants for all our meals: there wouldn't be meat on our plates without plants to feed farm animals. So when crops (food plants) wither, hunger and famine are soon on the TV news. Food and germs are deadly partners in other ways, too. Badly prepared meals can spread disease to all who eat them.

Starving families plead for food (above).

POTÂTO FÂMINE

A million Irish people died when a crop disease struck their fields in the mid-19th century. Many more moved abroad to escape the famine they called the Great Hunger. Its cause was potato blight, a mould that could destroy whole fields of potatoes in just days. It caused terrible starvation, and the weakened population were more likely to catch diseases such as typhus.

SOLVING THE PROBLEM

The starchy roots of cassava feed more African people than any other food plant. This plant survives with little water, even in poor soils. Diseases that attack cassava, such as brown streak or mosaic virus, threaten millions with starvation. Scientists at the International Institute of Tropical Agriculture, in Tanzania (below), have worked for ten years to improve this vital crop. By breeding the most popular cassava with more unusual varieties, they have produced a whole range of new plants. These resist diseases better, and they are also sweeter to eat.

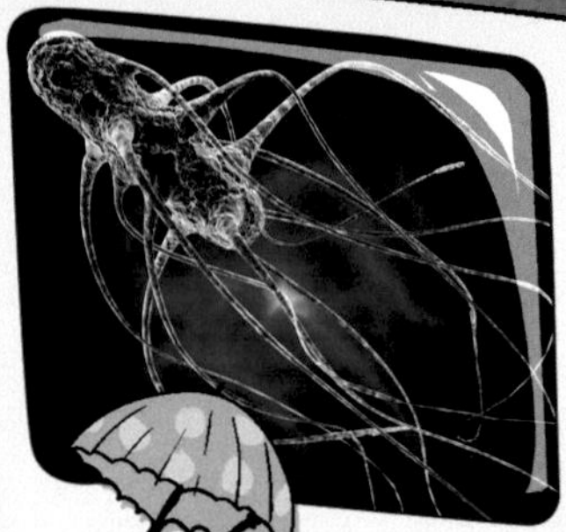

Salmonella bacterium

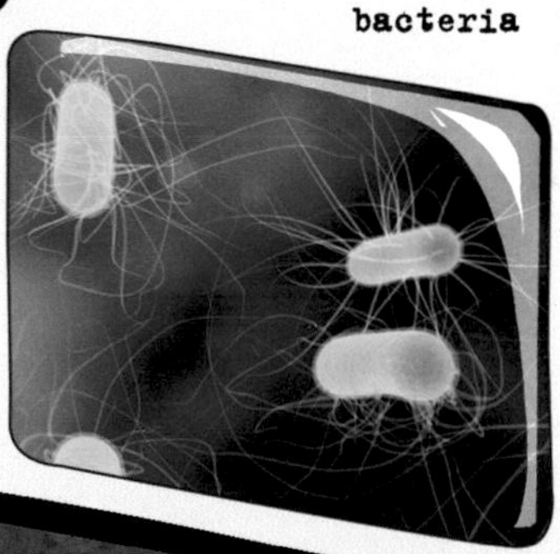

E. coli bacteria

THE TROUBLE WITH GRUB

In developed countries, much of our food comes from vast factories far from the supermarkets that sell it. If bad handling or storage introduces germs to food products, thousands may fall ill. Here are two of the main culprits:

SALMONELLA BACTERIA live in the guts of many animals. Eating them in unclean or badly prepared food can result in death.

E. COLI BACTERIA can poison us when we do not wash vegetables or cook meat properly. Like salmonella, they live in human and animal guts.

CROP DESTROYERS

Modern ways of farming can make plant diseases worse. A few high-tech crops, which promise big harvests, have pushed aside a wider range of traditional varieties. If all farmers plant these new crops, diseases can spread through them quickly, destroying the whole harvest. Food scientists urge African farmers to plant a wider range of traditional crops. So, if one fails, there will still be something to eat.

A 'black stem rust' infection on wheat stems

FUNGUS AND FEVER

Twitching and twisting on the floor, a frightened young woman grunts like an animal. She sees visions, and feels itching, prickling and bites on her arms. Three centuries ago, she would have been executed for being a witch! Today, we would know that she had eaten bread containing ergot. This red fungus grows on rye grain in damp weather. The frightening disease it causes is called ergotism, or 'Saint Anthony's fire' after the holy man whose bones were rumoured to cure it.

ERGOT'S ALARMING SIGNS

Ergotism takes two forms, attacking the body in different ways. The first form targets the brain and nerves – the body's communications and control system. The second form strangles the arteries that channel blood to our limbs.

SHAKING AND TWITCHING
As ergot damages nerves, sufferers' bodies twitch, and bend into unnatural shapes. They feel numbness and 'pins and needles' on their skin. They also suffer sickness and headaches.

SEEING VISIONS
Ergot contains a chemical similar to LSD – a drug also known as 'acid' – and its effects are similar. Sufferers may have hallucinations, seeing or hearing strange things that exist only in their minds.

LOSING LIMBS
When ergotism damages the arteries, it blisters and reddens the fingers and toes, then makes them numb. Eventually, it cuts off the flow of blood to the feet and hands, so that the flesh on them dies.

INFECTED GRAIN

Ergot spreads in the damp weather that ruins grain harvests. Anxious, hungry farm workers may overlook the black, withered heads of rye that are a sure sign of the fungus. Ground with the rye grain, ergot stains the flour red if there is enough fungus in the crop. However, rye flour is dark in colour, so the tiny amounts of fungus needed to cause an epidemic usually go unnoticed.

Ergot fungus growing on ears of rye

ÂMERICÂN WITCHES?

At the end of the 17th century, young girls in the village of Salem, Massachusetts (USA), began screaming, having fits, throwing objects and complaining of being pricked with pins. The girls and others in the village were accused of witchcraft, and put on trial – 20 of them were executed. Nobody knows what caused the outbreak, but some scientists have suggested that the rye bread they had eaten may have contained ergot.

A child writhes on the floor at the Salem witch trials.

BREÂD SPREÂDS DEÂTH

Ergotism was worst in Northern Europe. The heavy soil and damp climate meant that rye was the only grain that would grow there. Historians cannot count how many died and how often the disease struck – but they estimate that out of every five who ate the poisoned bread, two people died. Here are some of the most serious epidemics:

- **FRANCE, 922CE:** an epidemic of ergotism killed about 40,000 people.

- **FRANCE, 1128CE:** 14,000 people died in an outbreak in the capital, Paris.

- **GERMANY, 1374CE:** ergotism may have begun the crazed 'dancing fever' that swept through Aix-La-Chapelle (Aachen).

- **RUSSIA, 1722CE:** 20,000 died, including thousands of soldiers, forcing the Russian emperor to call off a war.

- **FINLAND, 1862–63CE:** a famine (food shortage) forced people to eat whatever they could find – and 1,400 caught ergotism.

MODERN DÂNGERS

The War on Germs isn't over! Here in the Pox Lab control room, everyone is still on red alert. Why? After two centuries of medical research, surely deadly epidemics no longer threaten our health? Unfortunately, they do. In a few ways, the dangers are increasing. Modern threats come from many different directions: from food, from warfare, and from the misuse of drugs. The biggest hazard of all is... people's foreign holidays!

GERMS ON BOARD

Modern aircraft bring every continent within quick, easy reach of travellers... and the diseases they carry. Scientists have long known that bugs hitch rides on planes, but it was only in 2003 that they realized just how serious the problem was. The first case of severe acute respiratory syndrome (SARS) appeared in China at the end of February, 2003. By mid-April, it had spread to 24 countries. Travel restrictions cannot stop diseases spreading – they only delay them by a couple of weeks or so.

WE CÂN'T GO ON EÂTING LIKE THIS!

Animals are sometimes farmed close together, causing diseases to infect them all rapidly. The processing of the animals for food, in factories, then spreads – to whole nations – infections that would once have poisoned only a village. In the 1980s, British people ate meat from roughly half a million cattle suffering from BSE (or 'mad-cow' disease) before scientists realized the danger to the public. Fortunately, there is a way of ending these food hazards. We could raise animals nearer to where they are eaten, on smaller farms, and in better conditions.

A large number of cattle feeding together in an intensive 'feed lot'

BIOLOGICAL WARFARE

About 3,500 years ago, the Hittite people from Turkey were the first to use germs in war. They drove sheep infected with rabbit fever into cities they aimed to conquer. It probably killed one in six humans who caught the disease. Biological weapons are still a threat today. Most nations have signed a treaty promising not to make or use them. Making large amounts of a deadly germ — such as the disease known as anthrax — is difficult and dangerous, but even small quantities can cause a lot of harm. There was widespread panic in the United States, in 2001, when five people died after opening anthrax-filled envelopes posted to them.

The internationally recognized 'biohazard' warning symbol

A Chinese medical worker disinfecting a passenger plane in 2003.

GO THE FULL COURSE!

Antibiotic drugs are our most powerful weapon against bacteria, but careless use can stop them from working. Antibiotics kill bacteria if the dose is strong enough, and the patient takes all the tablets. However, some patients share tablets, or stop taking them when they start to feel better. Then the bacteria don't die — or, worse still, they find ways to protect themselves against the antibiotics. An epidemic of an 'antibiotic-resistant' disease such as TB (see page 43) would be very hard to stop. So, if we want to continue fighting bacteria with antibiotics, we actually need to use them less frequently.

X-RAY RESCUE

To its 19th-century victims, 'consumption' was a slow but determined killer. Nicknamed for its ability to 'consume' (eat up) sufferers, the disease was incurable. The only treatment was rest, good food and fresh air – but these were luxuries that many people could not afford. Today, doctors call the disease tuberculosis, and they have tamed its frightening, deadly power. They can spot 'TB' with a chest X-ray (right), and usually cure it with antibiotics.

X-ray image of the lungs, showing TB's wispy shadows (top left)

COUGH OF DEATH

The disease has many symptoms, but the tell-tale sign of TB is coughing. TB bacteria destroy the lungs, and sufferers spit out blood. Most have a high body temperature, too, and pale skin. They lose weight, because the disease takes away their appetite. Before there was a cure for TB, wealthy sufferers recovered in special clinics far from their city homes. They rested in outdoor beds, soaking up sunshine and breathing clean, fresh air.

THE 'TB' SUFFERER

- Night sweats
- Rosy cheeks
- Hacking cough
- Weight loss
- Pale skin
- Uncontrollable shivering

BONE MARROW AND TB

Advanced TB kills blood-making marrow inside a sufferer's bones, causing marks that archaeologists can spot in the body, even after 3,000 years.

LOOKING AT THE LUNGS

In 1895, German scientist Wilhelm Röntgen discovered invisible beams that passed through solid objects. Named X-rays, they allowed doctors to look inside the body without cutting it up. Within two years, doctors had begun using them to make pictures of patients' lungs. Tuberculosis showed up as cloudy shadows. This was a quick way to spot TB cases – and from the 1950s onwards, many countries took X-rays of everyone at risk of the disease.

CELEBRITY SUFFERERS

Tuberculosis killed so many famous, wealthy and talented people in the 18th and 19th centuries that it became almost a 'fashionable' way to die. The 'Romantic' painters and writers of the age saw TB as a tragic disease. They liked to believe that it affected creative and artistic types more than others. In fact, the opposite was true.

Though TB claimed celebrity victims, it was more likely to kill the poor and unknown. Unlike the rich, they were more likely to be living crowded together, or in dirty, airless homes where TB bacteria can thrive. Hunger meant that poorer people could not fight off the disease as easily.

This is the mummy of Egyptian woman Irtyersenu, who died of TB about 2,600 years ago.

Napoleon II (1811–32) was French emperor for 15 days when he was four. He died of TB, aged just 21.

Lead aprons protect against absorbing too many X-rays.

Eleanor Roosevelt (1884–1962) was the very popular wife of a US president. TB played a part in her death.

The tell-tale scar of the BCG injection

RETURN OF THE KILLER

From the 1940s to the 1960s, researchers developed several antibiotic drugs that could cure TB. But soon, doctors found the drugs did not work on every patient. TB was developing antibiotic resistance (see page 41). Then, in 2006, patients in South Africa started dying from a form of TB that no drug could cure. Disease-control agencies now fear that the threat of TB may, in the future, be as great as it was a century ago.

Â JÂB FOR TB

Preventing TB is easier than curing it, and the BCG vaccine does just this. The second two letters of its name honour the French scientists, Calmette and Guérin, who developed the vaccine. (The B stands for *bacillus*, or bacteria.) Most children who get the jab cannot catch some forms of TB. Protection is not always reliable, though, and wears off after about 20 years.

THE FUTURE

What is the future for pox and plague? We try to control them. Preventing diseases is one way. Fighting them when they attack is another. New diseases are appearing all the time, and old ones that we thought were under control are returning to threaten our health. Viruses and bacteria mutate (change), so it is vital that people get the right information and take the correct treatments for them.

NEW WAYS TO GET VERY ILL

Monitoring new diseases at the Pox Lab is a massive task. Below, our crack team is tracking four: the Ebola and Nipah viruses, bird flu and swine flu. All four viruses come from animals — we catch nearly two-thirds of all human diseases this way. The two flu viruses are major pandemic threats. Ebola and Nipah are also very scary: they are often fatal and have alarming symptoms. Fortunately, they are rare, or strike only in very remote areas.

KEY

EBOLA VIRUS: began in 1976, in Zaire, killing nine of every ten people infected.

NIPAH VIRUS: first spread from fruit bats to humans in Malaysia, in 1999.

BIRD FLU: spread from chickens to humans in 2004, in Southeast Asia.

SWINE FLU: jumped from pigs to humans in 2009.

NORTH AMERICA

EUROPE

AFRICA

SOUTH AMERICA

Zaire (now Democratic Republic of Congo)

PANDEMICS ON THE RADAR

Most new diseases come from farm animals, apes and monkeys. So one way to predict pandemics is to check the health of people who hunt or look after them. They are the first to fall ill when animal germs spread to humans. 'Virus hunter' Dr Nathan Wolfe does just this. Global Virus Forecasting, which he started in 2007, looks for sources of disease mostly in tropical Africa and Southeast Asia.

Dr Nathan Wolfe

BEATING DISEASE

Developing treatments for infections, and vaccines to prevent them, is costly and difficult. However, you don't always need a pox laboratory to stop diseases. The best protection against cholera is clean water and soap; and a £3 bed net can stop a child from catching malaria. To provide these things, governments need money to buy them, networks to distribute them and people who understand how to use them. Sometimes, diseases mutate or are carried undetected in people or animals, which makes beating them a very difficult job. But science will never give up the fight!

THINKING GLOBALLY

No single country is wealthy enough to beat disease on its own. So, to support the world's governments, international organizations take the lead in controlling pandemics. For 60 years, the World Health Organization (WHO) has managed worldwide disease control. WHO drew up the International Health Regulations that aim to stop epidemics crossing continents. Many other organizations and charities work alongside them. For example, a charity founded by the Microsoft technology tycoon Bill Gates pays for health and education for some of the world's poorest people.

The emblem of the World Health Organization

ASIA

Malaysia

AUSTRALIA

POXY WORDS

antibiotic
A medical drug that stops infections caused by bacteria.

antibody
A protein the body produces in response to, and to protect against, a harmful substance in the body, such as a virus or bacteria.

bacterium (plural: bacteria)
Bacteria are very simple, microscopic living creatures that cause decay or infection in plants and animals.

biological weapon
A weapon that kills or injures by spreading deadly germs, or poisons.

cell
The smallest, most basic structure of a living thing.

contaminated
Spoiled, polluted or dirty.

diarrhoea
A health problem in which the gut contents become more liquid, and move more quickly through the body.

electron
The tiniest of the particles inside atoms. Atoms are the specks of material from which every object is made.

epidemic
A serious outbreak of a disease, which infects many of the people in the region where it strikes.

fever
A higher body temperature than normal, often resulting in heavy sweating and uncontrollable shivering.

flea
A tiny, jumping insect without wings that feeds on human or animal blood.

germ
Something other than a poison that causes disease or bad health: a protist, virus or bacteria.

immune
Unable to catch a disease.

infection
An invasion of the body by a germ, or the passing on of a disease from an ill person to a healthy person.

inoculation
The method of protecting against a disease by deliberately infecting healthy people with a weakened form of it.

microbe
This is basically just a posh name for a germ.

migration
Movement of people between countries or continents.

mosquito
A tiny, flying, biting insect.

mould
A type of tiny fungus that forms a fur-like growth on rotting plant or animal material.

pandemic
A serious outbreak of a disease, affecting several continents, or the world.

parasite
A plant or animal that lives on, and feeds on, another plant or animal — without helping it or killing it.

pestilence
A deadly epidemic or disease, affecting people or animals.

plague
A disease that spreads quickly and kills many people in a short time.

pollution
Spoiling — often of the air, water or soil.

prejudice
The dislike or unfair treatment of people due to their race, religion, sex or social class.

protist
A tiny, simple living creature, often made up of just one cell.

reproduction
The way that living things create more of themselves.

resistance
The natural ability to fight off a disease or infection.

sewage
Liquid and solid human waste from lavatories and dirty water from washing.

strain
An individual variety or type: bird flu and swine flu are both strains of influenza.

symptom
An outward sign of a disease, such as a fever, headache or skin rash.

syringe
A tube tipped with a fine, sharp needle, used to inject drugs into the body.

vaccine
A deliberately weakened form of a disease that, when injected or swallowed into the body, gives protection against the disease.

veins (and arteries)
A network of fine tubes in the body through which blood flows back to (and away from) the heart, which pumps it around the body again.

virus
A microscopic, lifeless germ that tricks the body into copying it, until there is enough of the virus for it to become dangerous.

INDEX

PICTURE CREDITS
The Publisher would like to thank the following for permission to reproduce their material. Every care has been taken to trace copyright holders. However, if there have been unintentional omissions or failure to trace copyright holders, we apologise and will, if informed, endeavour to make corrections in any future edition.
(t = top, b = bottom, c = centre, r = right, l = left):
Pages 5tl Science Photo Library (SPL)/D. Ferguson/ISM; 5tc SPL/Barry Dowsett; 5tr SPL/Eye of Science; 6b Shutterstock/Irina Tischenko; 7t SPL/Wim van Egmond/Visuals Unlimited; 7c SPL/Eye of Science; 7br SPL/Steve Allen; 13b Shutterstock/Biomedical; 18 Professor Shimon Gibson;
19tr SPL/Meckes/Otawa; 19cl SPL/ Dr Kari Lounatmaa; 19cr Reuters/Ajay Verma; 20 Art Archive/Eileen Tweedy; 23tl SPL/IML; 23bl SPL/IML; 23c SPL/CCI Archives; 23br Getty/Hulton Archive; 24 AKG/Musée d'Orsay; 25t SPL/James King-Holmes; 25c Art Archive/Culver Pictures; 25t AKG/Archiv für Kunst & Geschichte, Berlin; 27c Shutterstock/leospek; 27r Corbis/John Stanmeyer; 28 SPL/Dr P. Marazzi; 31c AKG, London; 31bl Getty/Science & Society Picture Library; 32 SPL; 33c iStockphoto; 34tl Shutterstock/Sebastian Kaulitzki; 35 Shutterstock/pcruciatti; 36 Getty/Hulton Archive; 37tr Shutterstock/Sebastian Kaulitzki; 37cr Shutterstock/Michael Taylor; 37b Alamy/Nigel Cattlin; 39l Alamy/Arco Images; 39r Alamy/The Art Gallery Collection; 40 Shutterstock/Mikhal Malyshev; 41 Corbis/Reuters; 42 SPL/Zephyr; 43 Corbis/SPL; 45c Getty/ J. Carrier; 45br World Health Organization, Geneva.